ANCIENT EGYPT

Connect the Dots & Color

Dot-to-Dot

Jean Joachim

Illustrated by Nancy Harrison

Sterling Publishing Co., Inc.
New York

For David and Stevie, who would like to travel the world,
and for Janet and Jim, who already have.

4 6 8 10 9 7 5 3

Published by Sterling Publishing Co., Inc.
387 Park Avenue South, New York, NY 10016
© 2006 by Jean Joachim
Distributed in Canada by Sterling Publishing
c/o Canadian Manda Group, 165 Dufferin Street
Toronto, Ontario, Canada M6K 3H6
Distributed in the United Kingdom by GMC Distribution Services
Castle Place, 166 High Street, Lewes, East Sussex, England BN7 1XU
Distributed in Australia by Capricorn Link (Australia) Pty. Ltd.
P.O. Box 704, Windsor, NSW 2756, Australia

Sterling ISBN-13: 978-1-4027-2880-8
ISBN-10: 1-4027-2880-8

For information about custom editions, special sales, premium and
corporate purchases, please contact Sterling Special Sales
Department at 800-805-5489 or specialsales@sterlingpub.com.

CONTENTS

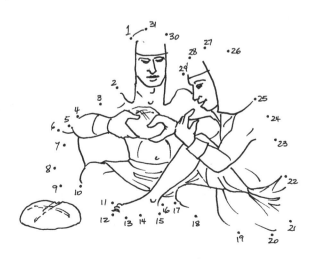

THE LAND

The Nile River, the most important geographic feature of both ancient and modern Egypt, flows north to south through the entire length of the country. It is what allowed the civilization of ancient Egypt to exist for thousands and thousands of years.

Ancient Egypt was divided into two regions: Upper Egypt and Lower Egypt. Lower Egypt was the northern part, near the Nile River delta and the Mediterranean Sea. Upper Egypt was the long, narrow strip of land south of the Nile Delta.

Upper Egypt has four different kinds of land with different climate and weather conditions: 1) The Nile River, which provided precious water for irrigation. 2) The floodplain, which provided rich land where most people lived. 3) The low desert, a dryer climate but still good for living. 4) The high desert, a hot, dry climate, not good for living.

The Nile River gave the ancient Egyptians political power because they had water power: water travel and rich land near the Nile that produced great crops and an easy escape from enemies on the Mediterranean.

Discoveries and Inventions: The first navy; canals (including the first Suez Canal)

THE NILE RIVER

The Nile is the longest river in the world, flowing over 4,000 miles (6,400 km). It was the lifeblood of ancient Egypt.

The river provided life in several ways. The Nile had an abundance of edible fish that provided food for the Egyptians. Its waters overflowed once a year enriching the nearby land and making it *arable,* or good for farming. The Nile provided water for drinking, livestock, and washing, too.

The highest ground of the floodplain is where most of the ancient Egyptians lived. On the floodplain they could farm, garden, and plant pastures for grazing cattle. The Nile's waters created fertile land in the otherwise dry desert.

The Nile was important for transportation, too. Ancient Egyptians created cargo, passenger and navy boats to transport goods and people long distances. The Egyptians respected the Nile, their source of life. It still makes life possible for Egyptians there today.

Discoveries and Inventions: The rudder–the part of a boat that goes underwater and moves back and forth, steering the boat to the left or the right.

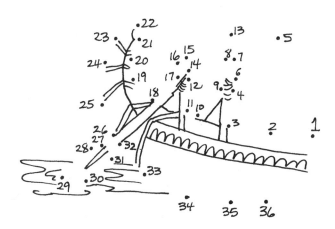

NATURAL RESOURCES

Quarries: The stone that was used to make temples and the pyramids that have lasted thousands and thousands of years was all mined in Egyptian quarries. Quarries were close to the Nile River. This way, the stone could be floated downriver on a boat to its final location instead of being hauled on sledges, which required the hard work of many men for many miles. Work in the mines was dangerous. At the quarries, miners built sanctuaries to Hathor, the goddess who protected miners.

Metals and Minerals: Copper was the first metal to be mined in Egypt during the Neolithic period. The ancient Egyptians figured out how to smelt, or separate the copper from other ores using extreme heat. We know this because smelting equipment has been found in the ruins of ancient mines. The copper was combined with tin to form a very strong metal called bronze. The tin had to be imported from Syria.

Iron ore was not discovered and used until later periods in ancient Egypt. Gold, however, was one of the first metals to be found. The special workers who refined gold didn't have to do any other work, like farming.

Silver was more rare than gold and was therefore more expensive.

9

FARMING

Farming in ancient Egypt began with getting and saving precious Nile River water for the dry desert land. Ancient Egyptians built reservoirs to contain water that overflowed from the river. They used this water during the dry season.

The Egyptians used a plow for planting and canals for bringing water from the Nile to irrigate the fields so plants could grow. Then it was harvest time. At the end of the harvest season, workers were paid in grain.

Grain was used to make bread, the main staple of the ancient Egyptian diet. The farmers harvested the wheat with wood and flint sickles. Then the grain was transported by donkey to the threshing floor, where cattle or sheep were driven over the wheat on the threshing floor to separate the wheat kernel out of the husk.

Grain was stored in grain silos built by the Egyptians. Later it would be milled to become flour to bake bread.

Discoveries and Inventions: The plow–at first it was just a bow-shaped stick dragged along the ground. The plow evolved to become a device that was hooked up to oxen, which made farming faster and more efficient.

Irrigation–by digging canals to direct the water of the overflowing Nile River, the ancient Egyptians created the first irrigation system for watering their farmland.

HUNTING

Ancient Egyptians hunted for meat. There were many kinds of animals living in ancient Egypt. Birds, gazelles, ostrich, and deer were hunted for their meat. Even turtles were hunted for their meat as well as their attractive shells! Pharaohs and noblemen hunted other animals, like crocodiles, hyenas, lions, antelope, and leopards, for sport. Only very brave men hunted these dangerous wild beasts. Men often hunted the more dangerous animals in groups because it was too risky to hunt alone.

While the pharaohs and noblemen and their families ate big game meat, the poorer people like farmers and tradesmen and their families ate mostly duck, goose, quail, rabbit and pork. The lower classes only ate beef on special occasions.

There were no guns in the days of ancient Egypt. Hunters used spears, arrows, throw-sticks, nets, and a boomerang type of weapon. Some hunters used chariots to help them in the hunt. The chariot would carry them faster over land. Others used dogs, like the greyhound, which were as fast as or faster than the prey.

Discoveries and Inventions: Ancient Egyptians may have been the first people to hunt for sport.

13

FISHING

The Nile had an abundant selection of fish: catfish, mullet, bolti, eels, carp, tilapia, moonfish, tiger fish, and perch were available for the taking. Perch, catfish, and eels were the most prized fish.

Woven dragnets and baskets made from willow branches were used to catch fish. Harpoons, pens, traps, and hook and line were also used for fishing. The hook was made by hand from bone. By the Twelfth Dynasty, metal hooks replaced bone.

Fishing could be dangerous. If the fisherman was not careful and fell into the Nile, he could be eaten by a crocodile or killed by a hippopotamus. The crocs could also take a fisherman's catch off his line.

Once the fish were cleaned, they could be prepared for eating in several ways: pickling, roasting, drying, frying, or boiling.

Fishing in ancient Egyptian times, like today, was also considered a pastime. Fishermen in the old days enjoyed sitting in a boat on the river on a pleasant day, waiting for the fish to bite.

Discoveries and Inventions: The metal fishhook–it evolved from the bone fishhook.

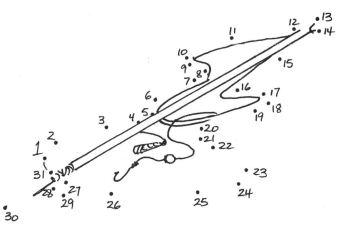

15

HARVESTING GRAIN

The ancient Egyptian farmer performed eight steps in harvesting grain:

1. The earth was plowed, or loosened up with a wooden ax. This was sometimes done with the help of an animal, usually an ox or donkey.

2. Then the seeds were sown into the plowed land by hand.

3. Goats were brought into the fields to walk over the land where the seeds lay. The goats' hooves pushed the seeds down into the soil so they wouldn't be eaten by birds.

4. The grain stalks were harvested with handmade *sickles,* sharp blades attached to a pole.

5. The grain was then bundled. Donkeys carried it to a safe, dry storage place.

6. Then the threshing process began. The grain was spread in an enclosed area and trampled by donkeys. The donkey hooves would help to separate the grain from the chaff.

7. Sieves made from reeds and palm leaves were used to separate the longer chaff and weeds from the grain.

8. Finally, the grain was stored in community granaries. Any excess was used in export trade with nearby nations.

16

17

MEAT AND FISH

Meat was eaten every day by the rich ancient Egyptians, but the poorer people only had meat on special occasions, if at all. The ancient Egyptians hunted meat and raised their own animals for meat, like cattle, antelope, and geese.

Meat was cooked over an open fire. It was prepared in some of the same ways we do today: boiled as stew and roasted. But ancient Egyptians didn't have refrigerators, so they had to either eat the meat while it was fresh or find another way to preserve it quickly. Egyptians used salting and brining, drying, or smoking to keep their meat safe for eating on another day.

Fish was an important part of the ancient Egyptian diet and was eaten every day. They ate mostly dried fish since drying was the best way to preserve fish in those days. Fish eaten right after the catch were boiled or roasted. Another way to preserve fish was to pickle them in brine.

The Nile offered a variety of fresh fish to eat: perch, catfish, tilapia and elephant-snout fish were some of the favorites.

Discoveries and Inventions: Marshmallows

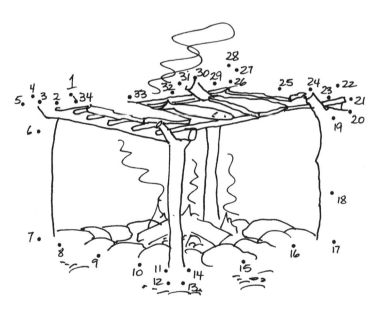

VEGETABLES AND FRUIT

Most Egyptians had a garden next to their houses so they could grow their own fruits and vegetables. Vegetables and fruit were grown year-round in the warm Egyptian climate and were important foods in the ancient Egyptian diet. Fruit was eaten fresh but was also dried so as not to rot. Jars of raisins (dried grapes) were found in the tombs of ancient Egyptian pharaohs.

Onions were a staple of the ancient Egyptian diet. Garlic was prized for its ability to spice up food. Radishes, cabbage, cucumbers, lettuce, beans, chick peas, lentils, and peas were also grown.

Dates, figs, and grapes were grown in ancient Egypt. Other fruit trees were imported: apple, olive, and pomegranate trees were brought to Egypt under the pharaoh Hyksos. Mulberry trees came from Persia or Armenia, while pears, peaches, melons, almonds, and cherries didn't appear until the Roman period of Egyptian history.

Olive oil was discovered from imported olives before the trees began to grow in Egypt. The oil was used in cooking, as a cream for the skin, and also to light lamps.

Discoveries and Inventions: Indoor lighting was achieved in ancient Egypt by the invention of olive oil lamps.

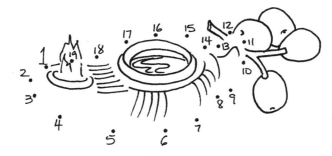

BREAD

Bread was the main food of the Egyptian diet. Making bread everyday was a lot of work.

First the grain had to be pounded and separated from the chaff. Then it was put through a simple mill that refined the grain until it looked more like the flour we have today. Then, after all that work, the dough still had to be made and the bread had to be baked in a clay oven! Bread dough was formed into loaves by hand and cooked on a clay disk covered by a lid. Later, a metal baking sheet was created. Egyptians who had no oven cooked very thin bread on the hot sand.

To keep bread interesting, different fruits and flavorings were added to bread, such as sesame seeds, honey, dates, figs, raisins, oil, or herbs.

Bread was used as payment to workers. At the end of the workday, wealthy noblemen paid their farm workers and other laborers in loaves of bread. A large bakery was discovered in ruins near Giza in Egypt. Scientists guessed that the bakery was big enough to make enough bread for 20,000 workers!

Discoveries and Inventions: Pancakes

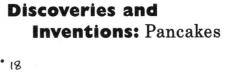

LAND TRANSPORTATION

Since there were no cars, bicycles, motorcycles or airplanes, people in ancient Egypt walked most of the time. Although there were no roads like we have today, the dirt that was dug up to make canals got packed down on embankments by traffic from people and donkeys, creating crude roads.

Litters, simple chairs sitting on strong poles, were used by nobility. The nobleman rode in the chair while it was carried on the shoulders of six or eight strong men.

Sledges were strong wooden platforms for carrying really heavy loads, like stone statues. The statue would be laid flat on the sledge. Strong men or oxen would drag the sledge by holding ropes that were attached to it.

Camels were brought to Egypt by invading Persians in the fifth century BC. The most common "beast of burden" was the donkey. Donkeys were used to help with farming as well as transportation.

Chariots were used only by pharaohs and other wealthy men. They were pulled by horses. Horses were expensive to keep and so were not as popular as donkeys.

Discoveries and Inventions: Carrier pigeons were trained and used as a way to transport messages over long distances.

WATER TRANSPORTATION

People sometimes waded across the shallow sections of the Nile River. In deep or wide sections, ferries were used to bring people from one shore to the other. The ferries, belonging to noblemen and the wealthy, carried poorer people across the river for free. Crossing the river had risks: hungry crocodiles and hippos were waiting for any unlucky person who fell overboard.

What about bridges? Bridges were rare in ancient Egypt and none was long enough or sturdy enough to cross the Nile.

Shipping was important to the ancient Egyptian economy because it enabled people to sell their grain, cloth, and other goods to other Egyptians living miles away or else to other countries. Rafts, boats, and ships were used to move goods and food up and down the Nile River.

During high-water times, canals were also used to move goods. A shipping canal was constructed between the Nile and the Red Sea, allowing boats and ships to move great distances looking for new markets for their food and merchandise.

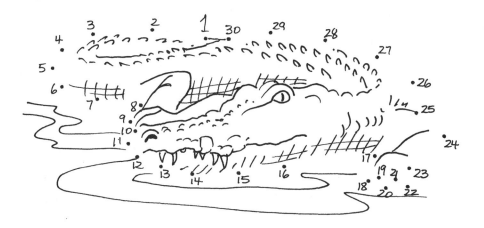

Discoveries and Inventions: The steam engine was invented by Heron of Alexandria.

THE CHARIOT

The chariot was a small cart with room for two men to stand. It had a little platform with two big wheels on either side. Two horses were hitched to a pole coming from the front center. The wheels were made of wood. Wheels were made by soaking wood in boiling water until it could be bent, then letting it dry.

The chariot was used as a method of transportation for nobility, for hunting, and for fighting. As a weapon in war, the chariot had its good points and bad points. On the good side, the chariot allowed two men to penetrate an enemy line quickly. While one rider drove the chariot, the other shot arrows at the enemy.

On the bad side, the chariot was not a sturdy vehicle since it was only made of wood. Oftentimes the riders would get thrown from the chariot if it hit a rock. If the chariot broke during battle, it stranded the two soldiers without a quick means of escape.

Discoveries and Inventions: The ancient Egyptians improved the chariot's design in several ways: they made it lighter, changed the axle position, and covered part of the axle with metal to reduce friction and wear-and-tear.

GOVERNMENT

The ruler over all the land was called a pharaoh. The pharaoh was considered to be a god as well as a ruler. He or she was believed to know the secrets of heaven and earth. Because the pharaoh was considered a god, his power was absolute.

The pharaoh was responsible for all aspects of Egyptian life: keeping irrigation going, commanding the army, keeping peace, and issuing all laws. By controlling the land, he controlled all trade, too. The pharaoh owned all mines, quarries, and trading fleets that sailed abroad.

The pharaoh had a second in command, called a *vizier* or Chief Overseer. The vizier carried out the pharaoh's orders, was a diplomat, and handled tax collection and public works.

Under the vizier were the governors, who controlled sections of the country, like counties. Under the governors were the scribes-writers, who kept all the written records-and the overseers, who supervised farming.

Discoveries and Inventions: National government

KING TUTANKHAMEN

King Tut, as he is called today, became pharaoh when he was only about nine years old. That is how old he was when his father died. Kingship was passed down from father to son. King Tut didn't really rule Egypt when he was nine. Other high officials made all the important decisions about Egypt at that time.

King Tut lived to be only nineteen years old. When he died, he was given a kingly passing into the afterlife by the construction of a tomb. His tomb is one of the few ancient Egyptian rulers' tombs to be uncovered almost completely untouched. We have learned much about life in ancient Egypt by the study of the artifacts, drawings, and writings from King Tut's tomb. Even though he only ruled a few years, King Tut is famous today because his tomb was discovered and so many things were found intact. It took ten years to get all the items out of Tut's tomb.

Discoveries and Inventions: The calendar and the automatic door

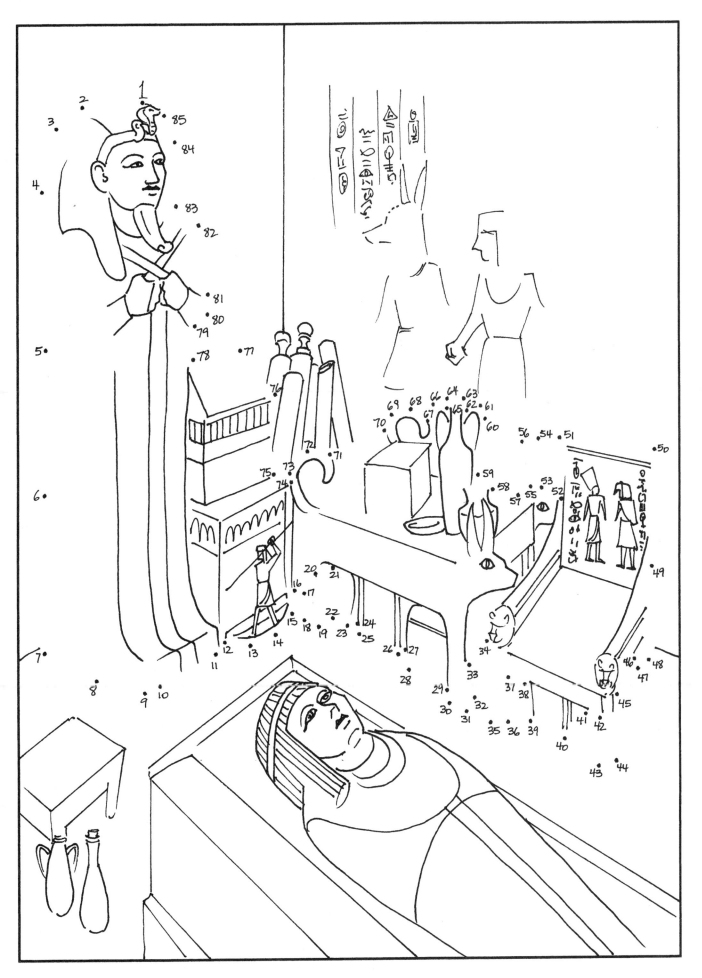

THE PYRAMIDS

The pyramids are some of the remains of powerful and amazing dynasties that ruled Egypt 5,000 years ago. The pyramids were built to honor the great pharaohs–the kings of Egypt–and to make sure that they had a smooth trip to the afterlife, where the pharaohs ruled as gods.

The Great Pyramid at Giza, an eternal tomb for a divine king, is made up of over two million blocks of stone. Some of these blocks weigh as much as nine tons!

Within the pyramids were chambers, and tombs for the mighty pharaohs. Each tomb contained the *mummified* or preserved body of the ancient pharaoh and everything he would need for the afterlife, including food, furniture, gold, and containers for water.

The pyramids took many years to build. One reason is because they waited for the seasons when the Nile was flooded so they could float some of these great big stones down the river to the location of the pyramid. Large bakeries were unearthed near pyramids. These huge bakeries baked thousands of loaves of bread to use as payment to the workers building the pyramids.

Discoveries and Inventions: The Great Pyramids

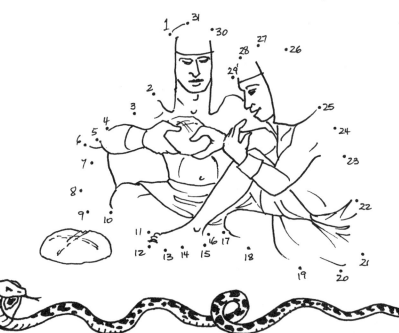

THE SPHINX

The Sphinx is a huge carving out of a giant rock in Giza. It is the body of a lion with the head of a pharaoh. The Sphinx is carved from natural limestone. Because limestone is not the hardest rock, the Sphinx has shown wear and tear over the years. Some of the softer layers of rock have worn away and some details of the Sphinx have disappeared. Some parts of the Sphinx have fallen off. The nose is almost completely gone. There are a few traces of the original paint. It is believed that when it was first built, the Sphinx was completely painted and was quite colorful.

The Sphinx is an awesome creation. The paws are 50 feet (15 m) long; the entire length is 150 feet (45 m); the head is 30 feet (9 m) long and 14 feet (4 m) wide. There are no burial chambers in the Sphinx like there are in the pyramids.

Archeologists guess that the Sphinx was built by the Fourth Dynasty king, Khafre. One reason they believe this is that the Sphinx lines up perfectly with the pyramid of Khafre at its foot. Also, it seems that the Sphinx was designed to look like Khafre.

The Sphinx is a great reminder of the power, creativity, and ingenuity of the ancient Egyptians who accomplished huge tasks despite primitive means.

Discoveries and Inventions: The Sphinx

36

FAMILY LIFE

The basic family in ancient Egypt was traditional. The father was the one who worked all day at a job out of the house. The mother was in charge of the household, including cooking, cleaning, and caring for the children. In wealthy families, there were servants to help the mother run the house and take care of the children.

Because of high infant death due to primitive sanitation and medicine, children were highly prized. Having children that survived was a great blessing to the ancient Egyptians.

With so few modern conveniences, family life could be hard. Wood was scarce, so finding wood for cooking fires was an important job. Ancient Egyptian women made their own bread and pastries. There was always work to do, from cooking to tending the garden to weaving cloth and making clothes.

The average age of survival for men and women was about thirty years old. Ancient Egyptians didn't have too much time to get their families established before they were considered old. Children were expected to take care of their elderly parents, which in those days was around forty!

Discoveries and Inventions: Table manners, birthdays, deodorant, shoes (sandals), lock and key, clock, toothbrush, toothpaste and cough drops.

CHILDREN

Life was different for children in ancient Egyptian times. Children worked at an early age. Their help was needed to make food, build shelter, and help the community to survive.

Young boys learned a trade or craft from their fathers or a craftsman. Boys from richer families went to school. They studied religion, reading, writing, and mathematics. Some girls were taught reading, writing, and mathematics at home, and went on to become doctors.

Young girls worked at home where they trained to cook, clean, and take care of the house. Girls learned to weave and sew since they were expected to help make clothes for the family.

When elderly parents passed away, the sons inherited the land. The daughters inherited all the furnishings of the house plus the jewelry.

Because people didn't live nearly as long as they do today, they married very young. Marriages were arranged by parents and girls married around the age of twelve while boys married about age sixteen.

Discoveries and Inventions: The doll-making industry, baby rattles

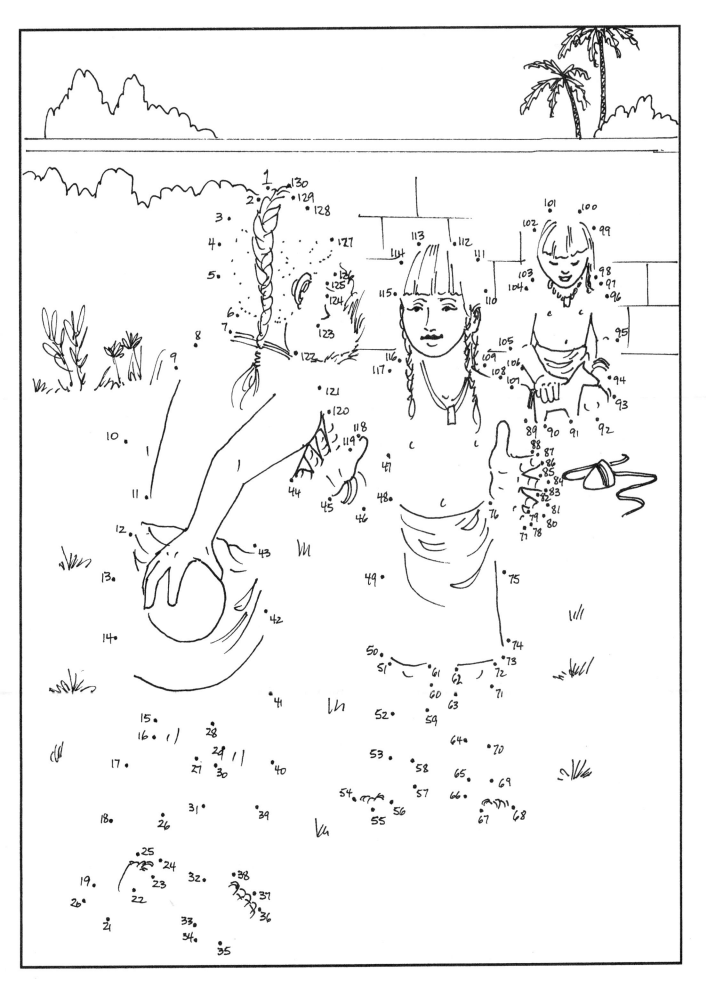

HOUSES

Ancient Egyptians built their houses out of mud bricks. The workers collected mud in leather buckets and brought it to the building site. There, straw and pebbles were added to the mud to make the bricks stronger. The mixture was poured into wooden brick molds and put out to bake in the sun. After the house was built, it was covered with plaster to make it last longer. Because these houses were only made of dirt, after a while they began to crumble. New houses were built on the rubble of the old.

A house's walls were often painted with designs or scenes from nature, like having wallpaper. Small windows kept out much of the hot sunlight, so the inside of the house was cool.

A typical worker's house had two to four rooms on the first floor, an enclosed yard, a kitchen at the back of the house—because it was too dangerous to cook in the house—and two underground cellars for food storage. The roof of the house had to be sturdy because the family often slept, cooked, and ate there, where it was cooler at night.

Rich noblemen had townhouses, two or three stories high.

Discoveries and Inventions: The master bedroom for parents and a system for air-cooling the home

43

FURNITURE

Ancient Egyptians didn't waste space in their homes with a lot of furniture. They didn't have many possessions to store, so a few chests and baskets were all they needed to keep their belongings tucked out of the way.

Egyptians didn't use tables often. They preferred to spread out on the floor when they had work to do, or use a wooden board while they sat on the floor or on a low stool. In this warm climate, the floor was a cool and comfortable place to sit.

Honored guests were offered four-legged stools, or collapsible stools with animal skin seats in well-to-do homes. Simpler people were offered pillows or mats spread on the floor. Low chairs were in use since the Early Dynastic Period, but they were reserved for the master of the house. Wooden chair legs were often carved to look like a lion's paw or bull's hoof.

Rich Egyptians and nobility slept on beds while the poor had straw or wool mattresses, a mat, or just the floor to sleep on. Beds for those who could afford them consisted of wooden frames on legs covered with strips of leather or cloth and linen bed sheets. Instead of pillows, headrests were used, made of stone, ivory, or wood.

Discoveries and Inventions: The canopy bed

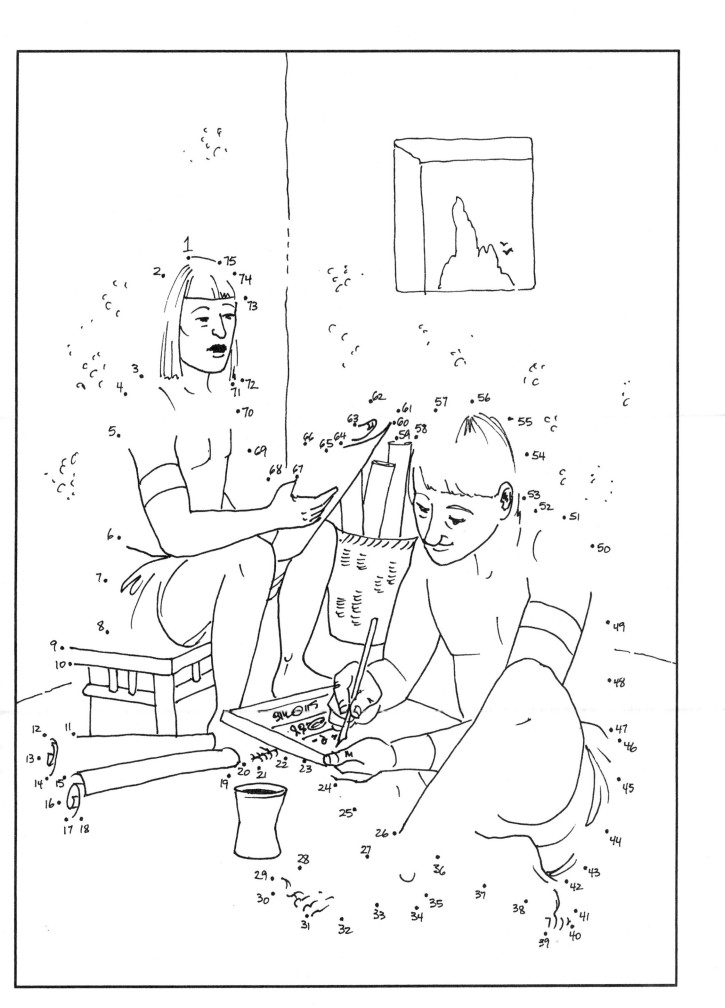

HOUSEHOLD TOOLS

In the days way before television was invented, the ancient Egyptians were very busy at home making basic tools and utensils from scratch, using stone and wood. They used looms to weave cloth from wool and flax thread they spun themselves. They made their own brooms out of reeds and their own rope out of plant and animal fibers or leather braided together.

Although Egyptians didn't own many things, they did need places to store the few things they had. So they built wooden boxes and chests with lids, weaved baskets, and made clay pots themselves. Food was stored in clay pots, linen bags, and baskets. Water was stored in clay pots, too.

Each household made its own knives from stone. Knives were used for cutting food, carving wood and bone, and trimming hair.

One of the most important gadgets the ancient Egyptians had was a fire-starter. This tool included a wooden bow with string, a drill stick, and a fire stick. The friction to ignite the fire stick was created when the two sticks were rubbed together very fast or when the bow was rotated quickly.

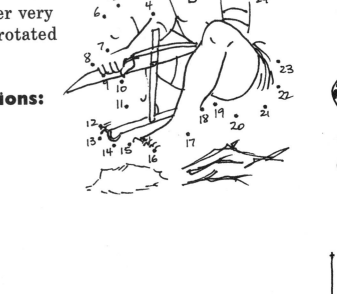

Discoveries and Inventions:
The loom and the fan.

TOYS AND GAMES

What did ancient Egyptians do for fun? Why, they played games! Games included sports games like hockey with palm tree branches used as sticks and pucks made from leather stuffed with palm leaves, to board games like Dogs and Jackals. This game was found in a tomb.

Senet is another board game that was found in an Egyptian tomb. It is a game of skill and chance for two players. Senet was played by Egyptians of all classes.

Children's games also included games like "The Kid Is Made to Fall." Two boys sat with arms up, while other children tried to jump over them. The sitting boys tried to catch their legs and make them fall.

Ball games were also popular with boys. Balls were made by stuffing a piece of leather with dried papyrus reeds. Marbles, one of the oldest games still played today, was invented by ancient Egyptians.

Children also had toys. Small wooden boats, baked clay animals, and rattles have been found in tombs. Many toys, like dolls and spinning tops, were fashioned from wood, bone, ivory, ceramics, and stone. Not everyone could afford fancy toys, but clay was available to make toys for children of all classes.

Discoveries and Inventions: Checkers, marbles, bowling, darts, Senet, and mechanical toys

PETS

Animals were important to ancient Egyptians as pets, for food, to help with work, for the sport of hunting, and as religious symbols of the gods. Pictures of animals were also used in art and writing. Egyptians kept dogs, cats, ferrets, monkeys, ducks, geese, gazelles, tame lions, and cheetahs as pets.

The most beloved pets in ancient Egypt were cats and dogs. They were well-protected by the pharaoh, who would punish or even put to death a person who killed a cat or dog, even accidentally.

Both dogs and cats helped with hunting. Dogs became watchdogs. Some dogs were so prized that they were buried with their masters when they died. Some cats and dogs were even mummified so they could enjoy everlasting life with their masters.

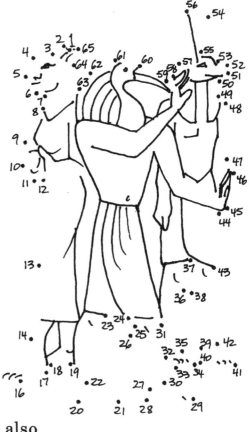

Dogs, cats, and other animals had religious significance, too. Bastet, a cat goddess, controlled the sun and had the power to ripen crops. Anubis, god of embalming, had the head of a jackal, a doglike animal. Geb, "Father Earth," took the form of a goose. He was said to consider geese sacred and gave them special lakes that also became sacred.

Discoveries and Inventions: Zoology, the study of animals

MUSIC AND DANCING

There was a large variety of musical instruments in the time of ancient Egypt. There were stringed instruments such as the harp, lyre, and lute; and percussion instruments like the drums, rattles, tambourines, cymbals, and bells. Wind instruments, like flutes, clarinets, double pipes, trumpets, and oboes, were also played in ancient Egypt.

Flutes were among the first musical instruments invented. The hydraulic organ was created using water pressure to deliver air to the organ pipes.

Harps were invented from the hunting bow. Tambourines were round or square and were used for religious or non-religious festivals.

Music was part of religious ceremonies. Good voices and the ability to play a musical instrument were highly regarded in ancient Egypt, as they are today. Singing and rhythmic hand-clapping were part of life in Egypt.

Dancing was a popular entertainment at festivals, religious functions, and parties. Dancers in ancient Egypt were often acrobatic and danced with great energy.

Discoveries and Inventions: Bagpipes, the trumpet, the wind organ, and drums. Ancient Egyptians improved on the instrument that has become our modern guitar.

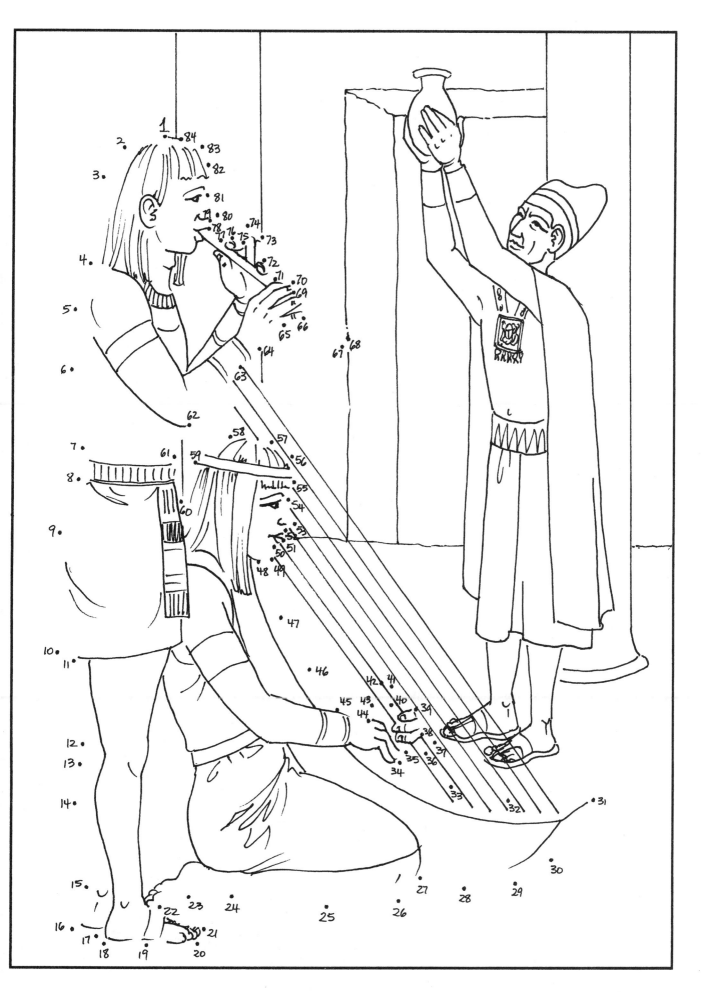

BEAUTY

Physical appearance was very important to the ancient Egyptians. Cleanliness was important, too. They bathed daily in the river or using a basin of water. They invented cosmetics and created perfumes, perfumed oils, and creams to improve the way they looked and smelled. Big beards or bushy mustaches were seen as dirty and neglectful of one's appearance, so the ancient Egyptian men shaved. Because soap had not yet been invented, the Egyptians used creams and oils to soften beards for shaving.

The Egyptians are well known for their eye makeup. Eye makeup came in green (from ground malachite) and black (from kohl). Tiny sticks of wood, bronze, or glass were used to apply the eye makeup. The black eye makeup helped to reduce glare from the sun. This idea is used on football and baseball players today.

Red ochre, a type of clay, was mixed with fat to create lipstick and cheek color. Henna was used to dye the fingernails yellow and orange. Creams and oils were used to keep skin soft and supple through the hot dry climate. Keeping their skin soft protected them from disease entering through dry, cracked skin.

Discoveries and Inventions: Cosmetics, beauty shop, and eye makeup

HAIRSTYLES

In ancient Egypt hairstyles were important. The hairstyles changed with a person's age, status in life, gender, and social status. Male children had a special hairstyle. Their hair was shaved off except for a long top lock on the side of their head called "the side-lock of youth." Boys wore this style until they were about eleven years old. After this age, many young boys shaved their heads. Young girls wore their hair in braids or ponytails.

Egyptian men wore their hair short, leaving their ears showing. In the Old Kingdom, women wore short, chin-length smooth hair. In the more modern times during the New Kingdom, women wore their hair long. Women decorated their hair with flowers and linen ribbons, and sometimes gold, turquoise, garnet, and malachite beads.

Wigs were very fashionable and were worn by men, women, and children. This gave rise to the business of wig-making. The best wigs were made from all-natural human hair. Some wigs were made with sheep's wool or vegetable fibers.

Discoveries and Inventions: The comb, hot comb, hair straightening comb, and wigs

INCENSE AND PERFUME

Why would ancient Egyptians need incense and perfume? Ancient Egyptian cities were smelly! Open fires used to cook food sometimes burned animal droppings. Garbage dumps were loaded with decaying food and animal carcasses. Human waste was not as easy to bury in cities. Incense and perfume were invented to mask these bad odors and make every place smell better.

Even if the Egyptians got used to some of these smells, they really preferred flowery scents and spicy, aromatic smells wafting through their city streets. Frankincense, a fragrant gum resin from a tree, and myrrh, a fragrant shrub resin, are two examples of natural products used to produce incense.

Flowers, roots, and berries were also used to create pleasing scents. Root of iris, bitter almond oil, cardamom, balsamon, oil of lilies, and cassia are a few examples.

Perfumes were oil-based liquids applied to the skin. Incense came in the form of pellets which were burned for their scent.

Paintings on tombs walls show us that flowers, berries, and resins were poured from a jar and then crushed to release their scent.

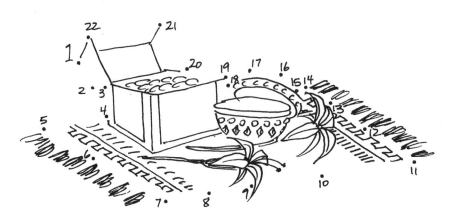

JEWELRY

Ancient Egyptians had a love for jewelry and an abundance of precious and semi-precious stones for jewelry, to decorate boxes, clothing, and hair. Everyone in Egypt wore some kind of jewelry–man, woman, or child. Rings and amulets were worn to keep away the evil spirits.

Both men and women wore pierced earrings, armlets, bracelets, and anklets. The rich wore collars decorated with beads or jewels. These were called *wesekh*. They also wore necklaces and pendants made of beautiful stones, like emeralds, red garnets, turquoise, lapis lazuli, purple amethyst, green jade, malachite, and carnelian. Quartz was also popular. It was ground and melted and became jewelry called *faience*.

Other jewelry worn by rich noblemen was made from gold or silver, which was more precious because it was rarer. Poorer people wore jewelry made of copper. Gold and silver were used for many other things besides jewelry. Gold was used for bowls, plates, and other utensils as well as necklaces and headdresses.

Some jewels had more than one use. Turquoise could be ground up and used as a pigment in paint. Jewels were used to decorate furniture, too.

Some jewelry, called *scarabs,* were used to protect against evil.

Discoveries and Inventions: The wedding ring

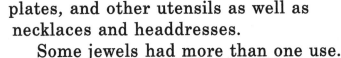

61

CLOTHING

The hot climate of ancient Egypt meant that the Egyptians didn't have to make heavy clothing. Clothing was simple and light, made from plant fibers like linen and cotton. Some wool was used and sometimes the rich imported silk from the Far East. Leopard and other animal skins were used by priests and pharaohs.

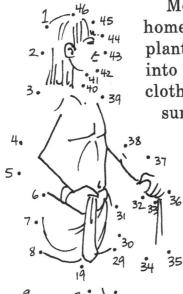

Most clothing was made by women in the home. The women beat and combed flax plants into fibers, which they then spun into thread. The weaving of the thread into cloth was done on crude looms with pegs sunk into the ground.

Linen clothing was simple in design: a long loincloth that looked like a kilt for the men and a straight dress with straps for women. Very little sewing was needed for these garments. Robes called *kalasiris* were created for both men and women.

Washing clothes on the banks of the Nile could be dangerous because of crocodiles. By 1200 BC there were boilers in washhouses where clothes could be safely laundered, rung, and beaten until clean.

As for shoes, sandals were sometimes used to protect feet, but people went barefoot most of the time.

Discoveries and Inventions: Scissors

TOOLS

Ancient Egyptians used wood, ivory, bone, and stone for their tools. Wood was used for plows, hoes, rakes, grain scoops, wedges, carpenter mallets, and handles for tools made of other materials. Wooden plows were sturdy enough because the rich soil near the Nile didn't need to be turned over, just broken up so seeds could be planted.

Stone tools were used mostly for cutting, pounding, and grinding because stone is harder and heavier than other materials. Sandstone and limestone were used for grinding while flint was used for cutting. Breaking stones to make tools was called *knapping*. It was a specialized craft because it was difficult to do.

Copper was used for tools, such as needles, saws, scissors, pincers, axes, harpoons, arrowheads, and knives. The softness and malleability of copper provided a way to make more refined tools, and to enhance tools, like adding a barb to a fish hook, or making smaller sewing needles.

When bronze was invented, it proved to be a big improvement on copper and stone tools.

Iron tools came later and had to be imported. Iron eventually replaced bronze for tools completely because iron is more sturdy. Bronze was still used for statues, boxes, vases, and other vessels.

Discoveries and Inventions:
Carpentry joints and metal piping

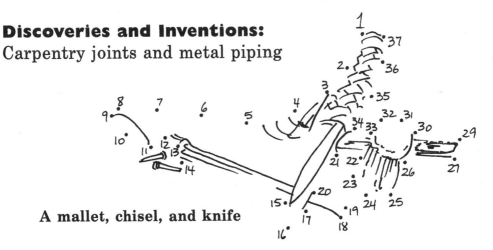

A mallet, chisel, and knife

64

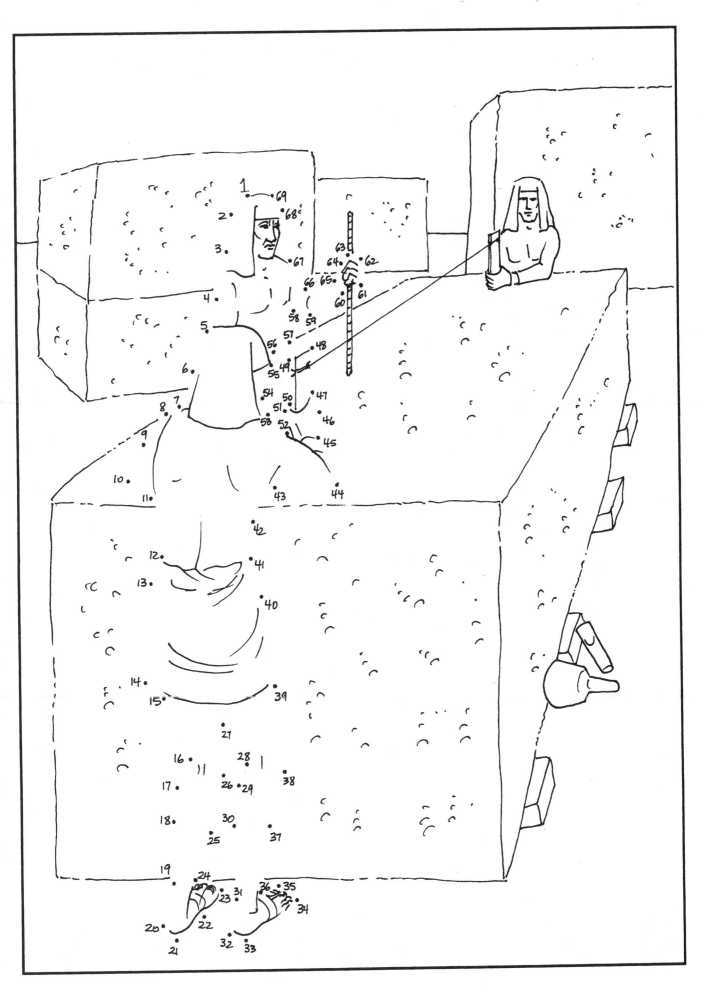

BASKETRY

Basketry has been around for thousands of years. It was one of the first crafts ever invented. Maybe this was because the raw materials necessary to make baskets–grasses, reeds, and plant stalks–are free. Basket-weaving provided lightweight, affordable, and sturdy containers for everyone in Egypt.

All ancient Egyptian households used plant parts to create mats as curtains on doors and windows, for sleeping, and to make baskets and bags for storing and carrying things.

Learning to weave baskets taught people how to weave thread into fabric. It also influenced pottery and carpentry. Even ships used basketry. The sails were made of woven papyrus matting.

Baskets were also made by coiling. A sturdy braid of plant material or leather was coiled around until it formed a three-dimensional spiral. It was then sewn together and a basket was produced.

What did the people carry in baskets? Peasants carried corn, servants filled them with bread, and builders used them to haul clay. Some baskets were made with lids, some with handles to hang or carry them by.

Discoveries and Inventions:
Botany and fiberglass

BUILDING IN STONE

The ancient Egyptians used several kinds of stone for building. Although igneous rock like granite is hard to build with, they used it anyway. It is very durable and has survived for thousands of years. They also used basalt, alabaster, limestone, sandstone, and pink granite.

The Egyptians had a cool way to split stone or separate a huge chunk from the rest. First they would cut holes where they wanted to separate the stone. Then they wedged really dry pieces of wood into the holes and soaked the wood. The wood expanded when the water was absorbed, causing the wood to split the rock!

The stone blocks used to build the pyramids were huge. These incredibly heavy loads were dragged on sledges.

To raise the blocks up to a higher level off the ground, ramps of compacted soil were built right next to where the stone was going to be raised. The ramps sometimes had to be very long so they weren't too steep to pull the stone up. This was hard and often dangerous work as a man in the wrong place could easily be crushed by the rocks.

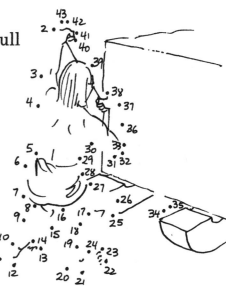

Discoveries and Inventions:
Architecture

GOLD AND SILVER

Gold was precious in ancient Egypt, but silver was more precious because it was rarer and harder to find. Craftsmen worked in gold and silver producing jewelry, dishware, pots, vases, masks, headdresses, and other decorative artifacts. Only rich noblemen could afford these gold and silver objects.

The gold and silversmiths worked while sitting on mats on the floor. They crouched over their work shaping, etching, and polishing the fine metals.

Welding and soldering were used to bond or join pieces of gold and silver together, especially to make jewelry. Soldering is the melting of one metal to join two other metals together. It was tricky because the tongs used to handle the hot metal were also made of metal. It was important that the tongs not melt before the gold or silver. These smiths had to work quickly.

One of the best examples of goldsmithing from ancient Egypt is the funeral mask recovered from the tomb of King Tut (see King Tutankhamen, page 32), one of the most famous pharaohs. Gold and silver were also used to make statues, furniture, drinking cups, and vases in royal households.

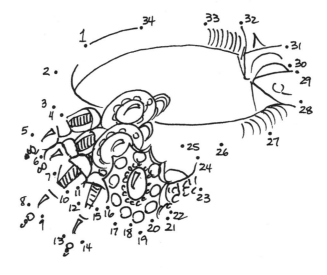

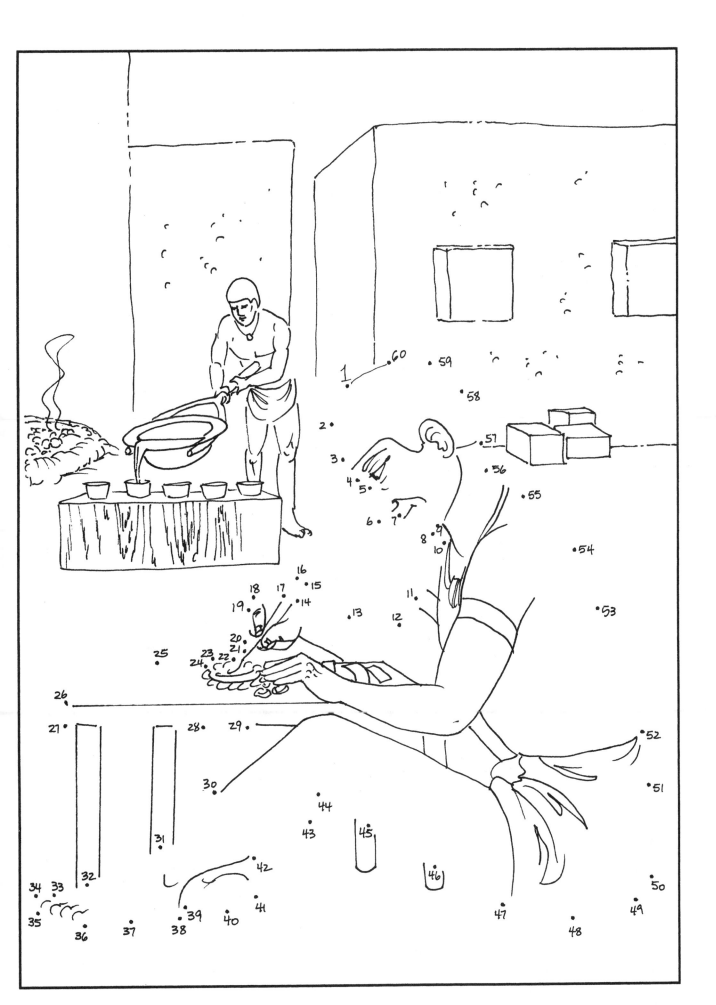

POTTERY

Ancient Egyptians didn't have cabinets in the kitchen, but they still needed places to store food, spices, and kitchen utensils. The first containers created by the Egyptians were bags made from fiber or leather, woven baskets, and pottery. Pottery is a special art.

Clay was plentiful around the Nile River so even Egyptians who didn't have much money could make pottery containers, toys, and jewelry. Clay was an integral part of the ancient Egyptians' life; they lived in it, drank from it, cooked in it, ate from it, carried liquids in it, and were buried with clay objects to take to the afterlife.

Most of the pottery was made from reddish brown clay found near the Nile, so it was called Nile siltware. A whiter clay, which was really a mixture of clay and lime, was found mostly in Upper Egypt. Higher firing temperatures were required for this "marl" clay, but it was more highly prized than the Nile siltware.

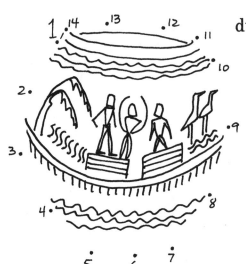

The potter's wheel was used during the Old Kingdom. It had to be rotated by hand. The kick wheel, where the foot controlled the speed of the wheel freeing up the hands to mold the clay, came about much later.

PAPYRUS

Papyrus, which was ancient Egyptian paper, was one of the most important products of Egyptian culture. It helped to transform Egyptian society with the written word. Writings on papyrus saved in Egyptian tombs enabled modern people to better understand the ancient civilization.

Papyrus comes from the Cyprus papyrus plant. It grew along the banks of the Nile River. Once the plant was harvested, the inner pith was taken out. This was cut into strips, which were pounded and soaked for three days until they became bendable.

The strips were then cut to the desired length and laid out horizontally on a piece of cotton next to each other and slightly overlapping. More papyrus strips were laid out vertically on top of the other strips. Another piece of cotton was placed on top. Then the papyrus was placed in a press where water was squeezed into the cotton. The cotton was replaced until all the water was out and the strips bonded together to form one sheet of papyrus paper.

People who wrote on papyrus were called scribes. Being a scribe was a good profession and was highly regarded by the people.

Discoveries and Inventions:
Writing, ink, and the postal system

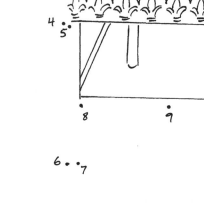

HIEROGLYPHICS

Before there was an alphabet, people used pictures to communicate. Ancient Egyptians used pictures, called *hieroglyphs*, "the words of god," to record facts and ideas. Hieroglyphs were used on papyrus and walls of tombs to record life in ancient Egypt.

Hieroglyphs were written in rows or columns. They can be read from left to right or from right to left. But how could you tell which way you were supposed to read the hieroglyphs? Just look at the way the people and animals are facing. They are telling you where to start reading.

Hieroglyphics are divided into different categories. The *alphabetic signs* have a picture for every sound, or letter. *Syllabic signs* have a picture for a combination of two or three consonants. And *word signs* are pictures of objects used as the word for that object. In other words, a picture of a bird could mean the word bird.

Colorful hieroglyphs were also used for decorating the walls of temples. For everyday writing however, a shorter version of hieroglyphs, called *hieratic*, was used. This was done so that writing could be done faster and ancient Egyptian history could be recorded more quickly.

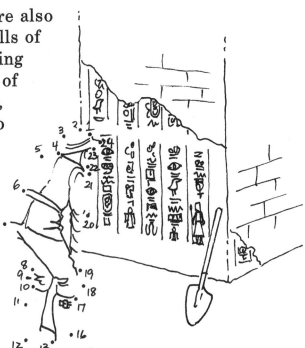

Discoveries and Inventions: The development of hieroglyphics began around 3,000 BC

76

MEDICINE

The ancient Egyptians believed that sickness was caused by a god, spirit, or magical force. Their doctors used magic spells and prayers as well as medicines to heal illness, broken bones, and disease. For their time, Egyptian medical practitioners like Imhotep-the famous Egyptian doctor-were very advanced.

Ancient Egyptians learned much about anatomy through the practice of embalming, the preparation of dead bodies for the afterlife.

The Egyptians believed in prevention, so they bathed regularly, shaved body hair, and did not eat raw fish or unclean animals.

Some of the herbal remedies used by ancient Egyptians are listed below.

- Honey was a natural antibiotic used to heal wounds.
- Aloe vera was used to treat worms, headaches, soothe chest pains, burns, ulcers, and for skin diseases.
- Camphor was used to reduce fevers and soothe gums.
- Onions were used to prevent colds.
- Sesame was used to soothe asthma.
- Thyme was used as a pain reliever.

Discoveries and Inventions:
Anatomy, antibiotics, embalming, surgical instruments, medical specialists, and dentists

INDEX